In The Name of God

TWO THINGS TO TUNE

ONE DREAM TO LIVE

Ali Bagheri

Main Entry	:	Bagheri, Ali, 1990–
Title & Author	:	Two things to tune one dream to live[Book]/ Ali Bagheri.
Publisher	:	Ganje Hozour Pub. , Tabriz, Iran, 2023
Physical Description	:	130 pages; 14.5 * 21.5 cm
ISBN	:	978-622-7975-45-1
Cataloging	:	CIP
Notes	:	Language: English
Subjects	:	Conduct of life, Success
Library of Congress Classification	:	BF637
Dewey Decimal Classification	:	1.158
NBN	:	9157038

Website address: www.ganjpublishers.com

Instagram ID: @ali_b.a.g.h.e.r.i

Telegram channel: @Ganjpublisher

E-mail : twothingstotune@gmail.com

Contents

Publisher's Preface

The valuable book of "Two Things to Tune One Dream to Live" written by Ali Bagheri is among important motivational books. Writing about such topics is effortful, and by reading this book you`ll find it unique and applicable.

We are proud to cooperate with Mr. Ali Bagheri in publishing this book. We hope that we`ve been able to make however small contribution to the spread of the mentioned topic in advancing the author's goal and to awareness of the people of all societies all over the world.

"It All Starts
With a Dream"

Introduction

First of all, congratulations to you for your success in overcoming excuses, taking a step toward a better tomorrow and staring a journey by reading this book. You may be someone who was looking for the key to success for long time, someone who was wondering why things are not going well while I'm trying so hard. Why there are people who can manage more comfortable life without too much effort, why some people are so lucky, why life is unfair. You have been studying and practicing for long time and you have mastered a skill and you are expecting to have achievements in return. There is something fundamentally wrong which is stronger than everything that you are implying and each time it's overcoming your hard work.

Let's look it this way, you are a driver, a soul gotten on a body for a ride and grabbed its brain as a steering wheel and controlling keys. You have taken very good courses about how to read the traffic signs. You know priorities very well. You know about driving rules, how to fuel up, how to maintain the engine, you know where you want to go and you got trained how to read the map and navigate. You are trying really hard and putting all these information in use, but you are not moving!!!!!

You are not aware that there is a hand-break up. If you lower that, then you will have chance to move forward. Then you will be able to use all those driving skills.

All I'm trying to say is that, it is important to know what is going on within you and having clear understanding of how your mind function, then you can use it to change things in outside world for you. Only educating your conscious mind and heading to your goals is not enough while your subconscious mind still has reasons to stop you, and yet you don't know why, so things are not going to work. Your conscious mind has not too much chance in front of your subconscious mind. So you better work on both and put them in same team toward your goal. So how we can bring them in mutual consent and make agreement between them about doing things. To know how we think and what happens when we are thinking, can help us to figure that out.

There are many forms of thinking, we can recall voices, we can hear or speak in our minds, we can picture things, we can imagine touching things, we can recall taste of food and we can imagine smelling things. Whatever we have experienced before, we can recall it mentally and imagine it. You can imagine taste of lemon and provoke your saliva but I doubt if you can imagine taste of a thing that you haven't eaten before. Simulate and create new things. There are two forms for thinking in which besides being able to recall and remembering, you can easily create new versions of it. Inner voice and picturing or we can say speaking and seeing mentally. So if with these two things (inner voice and image) besides remembering we can create new things, what do we create? What do we see? What do we say? Are they positive or negative? What is connection between these two things and subconscious mind? What is connection between these two things and our present feelings and vice versa? What is connection between these two things and our actions? What is connection between these two things and our future?

First words

İn order to transform your life you need to transform yourself. There is no sense in being the same person, doing the same things and expecting different results. For a few weeks as you start reading this book until finishing your main project, there will be some home-works, practices for you and also list of things you will do and things you will avoid doing. Afterward you decide keep doing it that way or you want to get back to way you used to do things. The main purpose of these home-works are to let you experience your life in a different way than it used to be. If you are not ready to take action and do the home-works, this book might not be helpful for you. Knowing and not doing has same result as not knowing.

"If we keep doing what we're doing, we're going to keep getting what we're getting."

Stephen Covey

The things you will consider and take action on them during this journey:

Discipline

Regarding further practices and exercises, it's important to be disciplined and not to skip anything in order to get expected result. So here are review and few tips about how to be disciplined. Discipline is to control your emotions, temptations and weakness from manipulating the rules and particular way of doing something, but most of us do not know that discipline is not something to apply in your actions or do it but it is something to become. You can't expect yourself having discipline on doing an important thing in middle of the day while up to that moment since morning you were a clumsy careless guy. Importance of tasks may effects your attention on doing something but when it comes to discipline, either you are disciplined on everything or you are not disciplined on anything. The good news is that you can easily practice and be more disciplined. Key is to practice being disciplined handling small and easy daily chores. It's like tuning a music instrument before playing. You like it or not, there is a quality connection between making your bed in the morning with the important task you will handle at work during the day. And also it is good to know this is not something discovered by modern psychology. When we look back at traditional life styles, trainings, costumes and etc...,we can find it. For example if you go to a Kong Fu school, first day, they don't teach you how to have 3 kiks on the air, they probably teach you how to stand or sit properly at first. Discipline was one of the most important lessons that one person should have mastered. Then something went wrong with education and then we as a new generation discovered that intelligent people sleep until noon, there is no importance in making our bed in the morning we will undo it at night again anyway, we have more creative things to do than organizing our place and we go to work with something like pajamas because of we are more comfortable and productive.

Diet

There's a drug dealer living in your brain and a medic as well. We think addicted people to drugs are only the people who smoke, drink or eat something, but those are not the only forms of addiction. Those are people who are addicted by consuming things externally. There is another form of addiction which I call it internal addiction. In this form of addiction you do not need to go to tobacco shop or drug supplier. External addicts get themselves to drug dealer to get something to satisfy their body and internal addicts provide their drugs internally. They starts to think about something negative so their brain itself produces drug so they satisfy their body. Yes you can get addicted to stress you can get addicted to anxiety. You can get addicted to chemicals regardless of where they have been produced, in the lab or your brain. Too many people subconsciously chose to live a poor miserable and unhealthy life because in this lifestyle they will get more of negative mental substances which they are addicted to. From now on when you reviewing a bad memory, thinking negatively or being full of hate consider that your inner drug dealer is poisoning you and with each consumption you are going deeper and deeper. So when we understand we can be poisoned from inside as well as outside, we can think of better internal diet as well as external diet. In first chapter, we will talk more about this but for now just consider that until the end of this journey you will have a diet you have to follow.

Regard that your relationships are also considered as your diet so try to clear your relationships and keep yourself away from people who have any negative impact on you. Anyone who makes you feel bad about yourself, they easily make you angry over nothing, playing victim, people who try to treat you in a way you will end up feeling that you are not good enough or any toxic relationship in any form.

No reviewing bad memory
No negative day dreaming including any drama
No anger for more than few seconds
No toxic relationships
No alcohol
No smoking

Daily

Physical exercise
Good diet: Fruit, vegetables.......
Meditation
Socialization
Enough sleep

No perfectionism

I always believed that one of the biggest obstacles of growth and also murderer of many dreams is perfectionism. No one grows unless accepting to change, no one changes unless accepting there is a demand to change, and there is no demand to change for a perfect person. If you want to grow try not to be a perfectionist because perfectionists are doomed to stay where they are and they prohibited themselves from moving forward in life. They cannot change to be better because they are already perfect.

Personally challenged by perfectionism and never started doing the things I had in my mind because of questions like, what if it doesn't work, what if it doesn't look good, what if nobody likes it, what if I make a mistake and etc. This book is not going to be edited and it is not supposed to be a perfect book. Thanks to software algorithm to auto editing dictation mistakes while typing but anyway there will be many writing and grammatical mistakes, so enjoy it. One of your exercise in this journey is to make a list of things you wanted to do but you never started because of thoughts like, you are not ready to do yet or any other perfectionistic reasons, then choose the ones which are the most meaningful to you and start doing it without questioning, editing and postponing. It can be start writing a, starting an Instagram page for business, you-tube channel, starting gym, learning a new language, and many other things. Remember the main goal of this homework is to accomplish it not to make it done perfectly.

<table>
<tr><td>

Table 1

1..

2..

3..

4..

5..

</td></tr>
</table>

Self-love

One things most of us has experienced and still we are having side effects of it, is used to having special treatment for guests. I remember that times when we were kid, in every house there were guest plates and cutleries, guest room, guest sheets and... . Best of everything should have been used only while having guest. This thig psychologically conditioned us not to take ourselves as serious as others, how do we look is more important than how actually we are. Years passed and this norm looked vanishing, but actually it didn't. It just moved to another phase. Now we do same things in different form on social media. How much our Instagram or Facebook page is similar to our real life? We are spending our lives to pretend and prove nonsense to others. It is time to say "f..k it I'm the most important person in my life". Others treat you the same way that you treat yourself. If you love yourself others will love you too, if you believe in yourself others will believe in you too, if you respect yourself others will respect you too and.... You are always the one who decides how things are going to be for you. Choose a person who you respect, care and love the most and write down how you behave to that person, how you take care and how you talk to him or her, which restaurant you go together, and every other things you do for that person. Then commit yourself to do all those things to yourself until the end of this journey and see what will happen.

Table 2

1...

2...

3...

4...

5...

6...

7...

8...

9...

10...

11...

12...

13...

14...

15...

16...

17...

18...

19...

20...

Commitment

Whenever you set a goal or make decision to do something, you are not gonna have the same motivation and drive in all the stages of it. Unexpected things will happen and effect your feelings. Things will happen different than you thought it would be. Priorities will be different in your mind. You will start to convince yourself to forget about the postponed big final award and get the small one right now. I always believed that mountaineering or climbing is more mental exercise than physical exercise. Especially when you go for long climbing as it takes few days to hit the summit. The moment will come that you are tired as hell, all in sweat, your toes are swelling, your legs and back are in pain. There is not too much to the top but also there is no too much energy left in your body. You look at the pick and you know how much more effort is needed to get it done, then you turn your head and look down to the camp and think about food and sleeping. That's where you really meet yourself. Your desire and principle are in a combat. But the pick of that mountain is more than just a summit. It's where you will prove to yourself your power of will, endurance and commitment. If you are not committed to what you are doing it doesn't matter how good your plan or goal is, you won't make it to the top. As you are reading first pages of this book you have to commit yourself to continue to the end and do all given exercises in the book. There is no meaning on reading and stop doing home-works.

Believe in yourself

Probably you have heard it a lot and it may sound stereotype but when we understand the reason behind you will understand the importance of it. Scientific studies shows that 95% of human brain activities are subconscious and only 5% is done by conscious mind. There is a lot to talk about subconscious mind but here I just want you to know connection between believing and subconscious mind. One of the things our subconscious constantly does, is to prove that we are right. No matter what it is, we will be right at the end. Your subconscious in some cases even tricks your conscious mind to fail doing something you could do easily just because you didn't believe you could do it. You are having an exam and you are constantly thinking about failing in exam, you go and take the exam at end of exam you realize questions are so easy for you and you have answers right. Results get issued and you find out that you have failed. You know the answers but you have put the answer ticks in the wrong boxes in the answer sheet. You may think that happened by coincidence but subconscious mind has its own mysterious ways to make that happen and prove you right. Remember that, the 5% conscious mind is not a good opponent for 95% subconscious mind. If you started doing something and you believe you are not good enough to make it done, don't worry that 95% of your brain is with you to prove that you are not good enough to do it. Vice versa is correct as well, when you believe you can do something no matter how hard it is, that 95% will surprise you so bad. Even later on you won't understand how you figured it out and things come together to get it done, you will just look back and say sh.............t. of course there are psychological reasons for it which we may talk about some of them in next chapters. For now just consider that you+95% subconscious+ 5% conscious = everything you ever dreamed. Most of the times you are worried about the circumstances that may happen in the further and that's because right now you can't see them in advance, but don't worry, you will handle them when it's time for it. If you see the first step and you believe you can take it, then for sure you are good enough to take next ones. Next challenges are unfolded version of the first challenge.

"As you start to walk on the way, the way appears."

Rumi

Vibration

Introduction

Before rushing to mental images and inner voices, let's get more familiar with our brain. What is going on inside of it and how does it function, what are inputs for it, what does it create and how does it vibrates out. The bitter truth is that we have never get educated about human being mentality. We have studied years and years of mathematics and physics but we never ever had one single course teaching us about mental health. As big author Robert Kiyosaki says "we have been taught the things that we need to know in order to fulfill the factories and companies". We never had a right education especially about ourselves. Whenever we buy a new device normally the first thing we do is to open the manual handbook and read how does it works and how we will use it. We learn how to use it before using it, but when it comes to our brain and mentality, we have no idea and yet we don't try to learn and understand what is going on within us. We only follow doing the things that we have seen regardless of being right or wrong. So first thing is to have a concept about what is inside the brain and how it works.

"Knowing yourself is the beginning of all wisdom."

— Aristotle

Brain structures

Brain is a complex organ that controls thought, memory, emotion, touch, motor skills, vision, breathing, temperature, hunger and every process that regulates our body. Together, the brain and spinal cord, from it make up the central nervous system. Most of its functions are done subconsciously without our conscious effort like breathing. Consciously we mostly use it for thinking (According to cognitive neuroscientists, we are conscious of only about 5 percent of our cognitive activity, so most of our decisions, actions, emotions, and behavior depends on the 95 percent of brain activity that goes beyond our conscious awareness.)

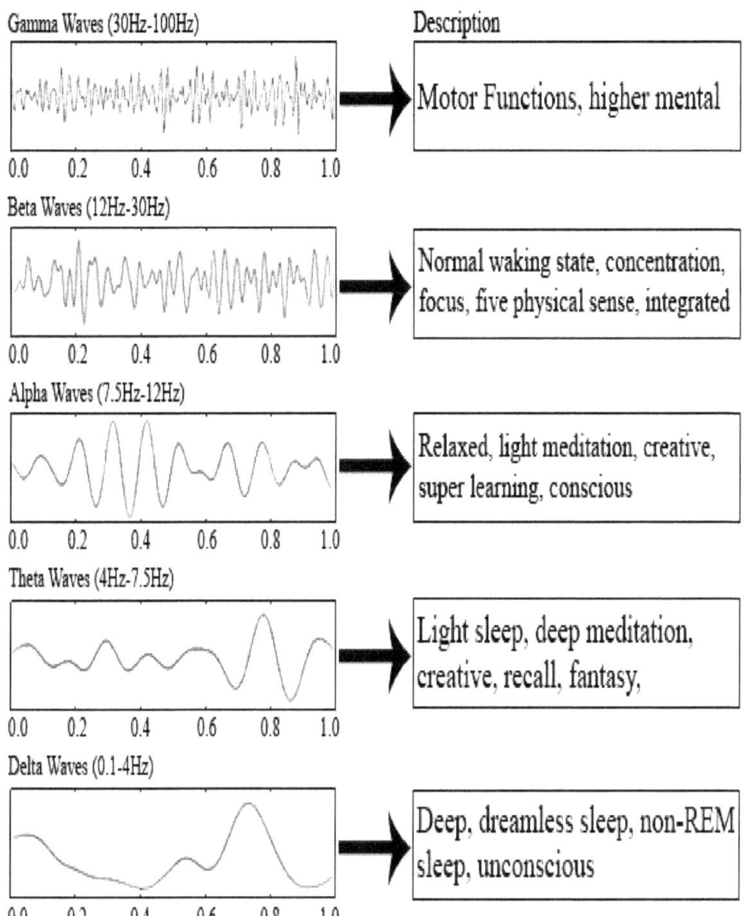

Gamma Waves (30Hz-100Hz)
0.0 0.2 0.4 0.6 0.8 1.0
Description
Motor Functions, higher mental
Beta Waves (12Hz-30Hz)
0.0 0.2 0.4 0.6 0.8 1.0
Normal waking state, concentration, focus, five physical sense, integrated
Alpha Waves (7.5Hz-12Hz)
0.0 0.2 0.4 0.6 0.8 1.0
Relaxed, light meditation, creative, super learning, conscious
Theta Waves (4Hz-7.5Hz)
0.0 0.2 0.4 0.6 0.8 1.0
Light sleep, deep meditation, creative, recall, fantasy,
Delta Waves (0.1-4Hz)
0.0 0.2 0.4 0.6 0.8 1.0
Deep, dreamless sleep, non-REM sleep, unconscious

Brain waves

Each person has 5 types of different electrical wave in his brain cortex, which is called brain waves. These brain waves are measurable. Each of these brain waves has a specific wavelength and a specific frequency, from the highest frequency (shortest wavelength) to the lowest frequency (highest wavelength) gamma (γ), beta (β), alpha (α), theta (θ) and delta (δ).

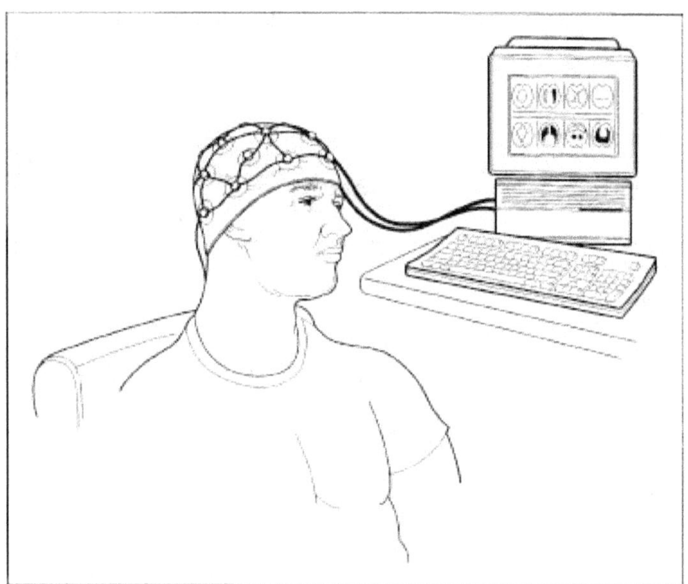

Function of brain waves and time

1. Gamma Waves

Gamma brain waves have the highest frequency among all brain waves. They are associated with high levels of thought and focus. They can have different effects depending on their levels in your brain: If your brain produces high levels of gamma waves, you tend to be happier and more receptive.

2. Beta Waves

Beta waves are associated with a state of alertness and mental activity. This is the brain wave you experience when you are wide awake and engaged in problem-solving or other mentally challenging tasks. Beta waves can help improve your memory and cognitive performance. When beta wave activity is dominant, a person is in an aroused state and actively thinking about something. Beta waves have been associated with a state of "mental effort" and are thought to play a role in concentration and focus.

3. Alpha Waves

Alpha waves are associated with a state of relaxation. This is the brain wave you experience when you are daydreaming or meditating. Alpha waves can help to reduce stress and anxiety. They can also improve your ability to focus and concentrate. When alpha wave activity is dominant, a person is in a relaxed state and not thinking about anything in particular. Alpha waves have been associated with a state of "mental readiness" and are thought to play a role in attention and focus.

4. Theta Waves

Theta waves are associated with a state of deep relaxation. This is the brain wave you experience when you are in a light sleep or drifting off to sleep. Theta waves can help improve your mood and reduce stress levels. When theta wave activity is dominant, a person is in a state of deep relaxation and not thinking about anything in particular. Theta waves have been associated with a state of "mental creativity" and are thought to play a role in imagination and intuition.

5. Delta Waves

Delta waves are associated with a state of deep sleep. This is the brain wave you experience when you are in a deep, restful sleep. Delta waves can help improve your immune system and reduce stress levels. When delta wave activity is dominant, a person is in a very deep sleep and not dreaming.

Delta waves have been associated with a state of "physical healing" and are thought to play a role in tissue repair and regeneration.

How to Stimulate Different Brain Waves

There are many different ways to stimulate different brain waves. Some methods are more effective than others. Here are some of the most popular methods:

1. Meditation

Meditation is one of the most effective ways to stimulate alpha and theta brain waves. Meditation helps to quiet the mind and allows you to focus on the present moment. There are many different types of meditation, so find one that works best for you.

2. Brainwave Entrainment

Brainwave entrainment is a method of stimulating brain waves using audio or visual cues. This method is often used to help people meditate or achieve deep sleep. There are many different brainwave entrainment products available, so find one that works best for you.

3. Biofeedback

Biofeedback is a method of using feedback to train your brain waves. This method can be used to help people with stress, anxiety, and sleep disorders. There are many different biofeedback devices available, so find one that works best for you.

4. Exercise

Exercise is a great way to stimulate all types of brain waves. Exercise helps to increase blood flow to the brain and can improve cognitive function. Find an exercise that you enjoy and make it part of your daily routine.

5. Music

Music is a powerful tool that can be used to stimulate different brain waves. Different types of music can have different effects on the brain. Find the type of music that works best for you and listen to it often.

6. Theta Burst Stimulation

Theta burst stimulation is a method of stimulating the brain with bursts of electrical energy. This method is often used to treat depression and anxiety.

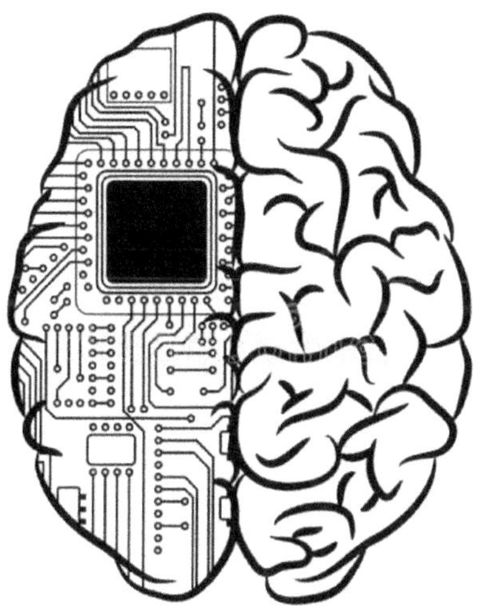

Read The Manual First

Based on personal experience and continuous information upgrading about telephone network and mobile phones, no matter we are holding PhD in electric or not, we all understand clearly that the cellphone do transaction to antennas connected to telephone network. We cannot see and hear the signal but yet we understand it. In some therapies there is device used which is called EEG (electroencephalogram). EEG measures our brain waves and shows electromagnetic activities in our brain and helps to investigate some mental disease. So cellphone is not only device with us broadcasting signals out, our brain does the same, it's creating signals whenever we are thinking and transfers it to universe and everything in it created by energy. First receiver is our own body. Cell by cell gets effected. Regard that when your brain is transmitting positive signals, is open to receive the positive signals, when it is in negative transmission it's sending and receiving negative signals. There are many things to go through about signals created and resonated by brain into universe but in this book we will focus on its effect on us and our lives.

What happens when we are thinking?

Scientists say when we are thinking, neurons release brain chemicals, known as neurotransmitters, which generate these electrical signals in neighboring neurons. The electrical signals propagate like a wave to thousands of neurons, which leads to thought formation. One theory explains that thoughts are generated when neurons fire. In other words in means that whatever you think is going to be formed as chemical in your brain. If it ends up with good chemicals you would feel good and if it ends up with bad chemicals you would feel bad. What do I mean by good chemicals and bad chemicals? We can also say balanced chemicals and imbalanced chemicals. Based on what we feed ourselves physically and mentally, activities we have mentally and physically, our glands in body and brain produce hormones and chemical messengers. All of these substances are produced for a reason and only the right dosage of it is needed in order to feel ok. For example Serotonin, Endorphins, Oxytocin and Dopamine are known as happy hormones. Having these hormones makes you feel happy but it doesn't mean as much as amount of these hormones increase in your body that much more you will be happier. Lack of dopamine can lead to disease like depression and having too much of it can lead to disease like ADHD. You just need the right dosage to be ok. This applies for all hormones. Cortisol can repair and protect tissues and also it can cause stress. When we are abuse drug internally or externally, we disarrange chemical balance in our blood stream. So regarding this, as same as we can be poisoned by what we eat or drink, we can be poisoned and get sick to death by thinking negatively. Actually most of the disease human being is dealing with it, is caused by stress-full life not poisoned food or drink.

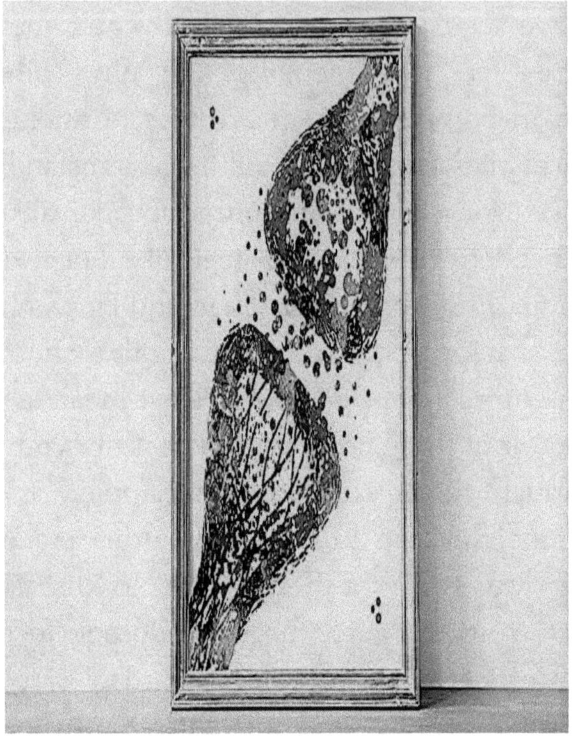

It worth mentioning that there is another factor between input and output of our brain which we know it as believe system. Thinking about certain topic can produce different feelings for two person based on their belief system. Barbecue for example, someone can feel craving for it believing as it is a delicious food some vegan can think of it as a dead animal being cooked and feel bad about it. Your believe system decides which glands to provoke or what hormone or chemical to produce in your body which will finally define your feeling. It is good to know that it can be compounded. It means that your current chemistry will effect mind and next release, so if you are in negative mode or negative feeling, you are probably going to create more negative results by staying in that loop.

Your thoughts are not just thoughts they are possibilities, plans and directions.

We read all these information about brain to remind that whenever we think we create electrical activities and we consume energy for that. Our body may be still but it doesn't mean we are not doing anything or we are not having energy consuming activity. When we are doing something physical either mentally, we consume energy and in both we can have productive or distractive results. If you think it's not good to jump off the cliff, don't jump off the cliff in your daydreams as well.

Your actions are result of your choses between different mental previews of your action. You imagine few scenarios and then you choose one of them to take action on them. Sometimes this decision is made by your subconscious mind. What options did you put on the table for your subconscious mind?

Every thought is a possibility so be careful what you are doing to yourself in your in your imagination. Only few of your thoughts get physical form and they are chosen from available options, so make sure that all you have in mind is good and productive.

Your thoughts effect your physic and vice versa

Have you ever noticed that when you're feeling stressed or depressed about something, you tend to hunch down with shoulders rolled inward? This posture generally signifies that your body is in protection mode. But something you may not have noticed, is that even if you're not experiencing stress, you may still be practicing bad posture, which can in fact change your mood in a negative way. There is something called Embodied Cognition. Embodied Cognition is a form of communication between your mind and body, and works both ways to send signals. From body to the brain, and signals from brain to the body. In simpler terms, how your body is positioned can directly impact your mood and vice versa.

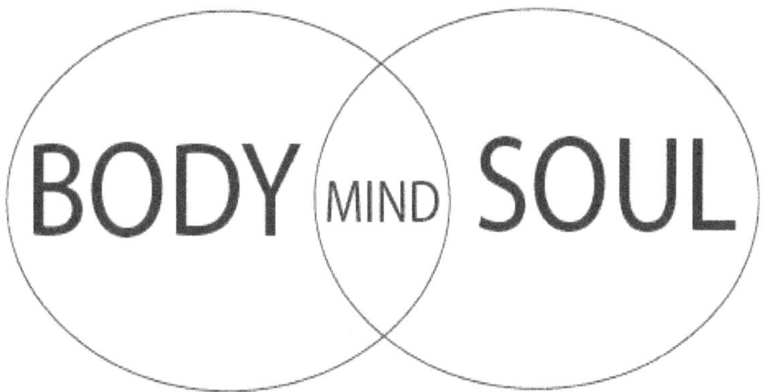

Positive Benefits of Good Posture on Mood

When we practice good posture, there are a whole host of positive benefits that impact both our body and our mind.

Confidence

Studies show that people who sit up straight with good posture have a lot more confidence than those who don't. In people who tend to slouch for whatever reason, confidence seems to be low. These studies looked at what changes occurred in a person's mood when they simply sat up straight and tall – increased confidence. Embodied Cognition can be paralleled with a simply study that put one person on a regular height chair, and one on a higher stool. The person on the stool felt taller and was able to see more of their surroundings, thereby giving them a feeling of confidence.

Self-Esteem

People who have low self-esteem can often tend to slouch with shoulders rolled inwards as a way of protecting themselves. In many cases, this is a self-esteem issue, as the person doesn't feel confident enough to be 'tall and proud'. Yet again, when they made this simple change, self-esteem began to improve.

Personal Empowerment

One study took two groups of students, one group asked to sit up straight, and the other to slouch down in their seats. A series of questions were posed to each group about how they felt they were doing in their studies and future prospects for their careers. The students in the first group felt that they were excelling at school, and would eventually lead fulfilling careers in their chosen field. The second group, the Slouching group, mainly felt they were only performing 'adequately', and were unsure of how things would go once they were finished school.

Awareness and Alertness

When a person is slouched down, they tend to not to be as aware and alert as those who practice good posture. Those who practice good posture tend to be more aware of their surroundings, more alert, and generally more involved in what is going on around them, which leads to a sense of belonging, vs. feeling somewhat 'outside' the fray.

Hormonal Changes

We all know that stress is a killer. And while poor posture due to stress is common, studies show that making the simple change of sitting up straight and tall can reduce cortisol levels (cortisol is commonly referred to as 'the stress hormone), which will lead to reduced stress, and the person feeling much better in general.

Increased Energy

In yet another study, results showed that those who suffered from poor posture had much lower energy levels than those who had good posture. When the body is in a prone position, other systems within the body can tend to slow down, including breathing, heart rate, and adrenalin levels. Conversely, when sitting upright and alert, the body and mind are running at much higher levels, leading to an increase in energy.

How to keep this muscle strong

Jim Kwik: Author of limitless and creator of many master courses for brain and memory improvement has few simple tips for having a sharper mind.

1. A good Brain diet. Eat the right foods to get your mind healthy.

2. Get rid of automatic negative thoughts. Make sure you are talking positive to yourself.

3. Exercise. Make sure you move to stimulate your mind.

4. Brain Nutrients. Find out what could help you personally in this manner.

5. Positive peer group. How are those around you helping you engage and encouraging you onward.

6. Clean Environment. How do you look after your workspaces and organize yourself.

7. Sleep. This is very important to help relieve and restore your brain to a healthy state.

8. Brain protection. Both physically in the lifestyles we lead but also from the digital age we live in now.

9. New Learnings. Constantly learn new things each day to keep your brain stimulated.

10. Stress management. When you stress, you can't concentrate on what you need to and overload your brain.

Vocal Vibration

Introduction

This is how story went. I'm in my home country living an ordinary life doing something that doesn't make me feel excited about it. I barely could say the difference between each passing day. Once in a while I find a way to get out of it and try something new in different city or country but not all attempts were successful. After last draw-back regarding COVID pandemic and sitting at home country doing my engineering job. I felt getting normalized again if you know what I mean. I googled couple things then I booked my ticket after that I resigned some accounts in recruiting websites and I got prepared to go for adventure. I flew to Istanbul and started looking for a job. The first interview I attended I got accepted but I didn't know what really the job is about. I started my first day with some training how to talk on the phone with client, how to convince them and blahblah. It was a telemarketing position. I used to attend project meetings and customer meetings in my previous job and I was a little bit confident about my negotiation skills. So I was thinking when the training ends I'm gonna start shooting on the phone and I will be damn good at doing it. But it turned out it is not as how I thought it would be. There were something different I couldn't figure out what it is. I was studying beside working and trying to improve myself in this job that lead me to learn some really life changing truth. It's only first few seconds of call which will determine that client wants to hear more or wants to end conversation with any excuse. And in this first few seconds my voice is alone. No body-language, no eye contacts, no previous recognition. All these times my voice was hiding behind my body language but now it's on its own. It seems that it's not doing very well. Then I keep looking for it and it turned out there is something called vocal personality or character.

People judge you by how you sound and how you look and if you are on the phone, the only factor to be judged by, is the voice. It probably happened to you as well when you know someone only on the phone, you have never seen them, and finally you meet them. You say to yourself, I didn't though he or she would look like this. You had different expectations form their appearance. We save characters in our mind with their voice and image. İf we are adding a character to our mind and we only have voice for them, we will create an imaginary image until we meet and replace it with original one. Sometimes there is too much difference between these two images and that's when we say I didn't thought you would look like this. Some people have huge difference between how do they look and how do they sound. You may have seen a bulky huge guy expecting to hear a deep voice from him but when he started to talk you heard a squeaky pitch that changed your thoughts about him. Why this happens? What are things effecting vocal character? What are other aspects of vocal character?

This research went beyond negotiation skills and lead to deeper findings. I found out very small portion of it depends on physical elements. It's more effected by psychological reasons. Form and position of certain muscles in respiratory system, throat and mouth define the tune and color of your voice. Form of the muscle are controlled mainly by your subconscious mind. The same way your breath, heart-beat, blinking etc is controlled by your subconscious mind. Actually, if your conscious mind controls them, you would have no consciousness left to deal with outside world. You will spend all to maintain your body activities. Some of psychological conditions affect us for so long time, especially in very young ages that causes long term trace. It had impact on shaping our vocal chords while we were growing as well. So it has left a long term effects on our vocal character. We have been using wrong pitch for long time that it turned to be the default mood. We got used to it and made it our vocal character.

So to maintain good voice and image we need to maintain a good psychological mood. What do we need to maintain a good mental mood? Your positive inner voice and positive imagination will increase mental condition, and then your mental condition will improve your outer voice and body posture. Destructive self-talk and self-image will reduce your confidence and self-esteem and finally you will end up speaking with shivering voice, slouching and terrified of being seen.

Imagine you are in a party with your friends suddenly one person enters to your table or circle in the party. All your friends know that person except you. Time comes to you to have a conversation with that person. How do you decide to how much friendly talk with that person or how formal to do it. Probably you will do as same as your friends did, you will speak with that person as warm as your friend talked with. Or if your friends didn't welcome him or her, you will have a reluctant tone as well. What if your friends are having wrong attitude toward that person. Maybe there has been a misunderstanding between them. What if I tell you sometimes that person is you and yourself stand aside and let others define your value by their parameters. Then you behave the way they behaved with you. You believe in yourself as much as they believe in you. Finally you talk with yourself the way they talked with you. Finally you end up with a poor, negative and destructive inner voice. Judging yourself by others wrong concept about you, can have negative impact on you.

Another thing giving the same result is to judging yourself with wrong parameters .It's reminding a story of different animals in jungle going through a competition with different sports. Imagine a turtle attending a running race with cheetah, or climbing between elephant and monkey. Is it fair if we blame a turtle for being slow and not considering it's defense mechanism, as amphibian, living in sea and land. What do you think about a turtle who is not confidence because it cannot run? Who put this idea in turtles mind? Other turtles who cannot run as well? What if you have no number skills at all, insisting to be a mathematician and finally you have come to this believe, that you are not intelligent. It doesn't matter you are very good in many other thing.

Danger of self-blame

Blaming yourself for what you are not, what you are not supposed to do and making it scale for evaluating yourself for everything. Do you blame people whom you care about, when they make a mistake or you encouraging them to do better next time? If you don't blame them, why do you blame yourself? Don't you care about yourself? Each time you blame yourself, you deepening the habit of self-blame. If you work hard on this habit, you will get to the point that in cold winter day, you will blame yourself for terrible weather. You find something to blame yourself for. This habit will turn into your main inner voice and that's a disaster. But how to stop this?

Watch your self-talk

There are words that marketers and business people never use because they are aware that two or more words can have the same meaning but they cannot imply the same feelings. If you are in a business and for a client who is in the budget you can offer another option by saying "I have a cheaper option for you" and also you also can say "I have a more economic option for you". Both of these sentences clarify the lower price for new option. First sentence saying "I have cheaper option for you" means you can have another option with lower price and lower quality. Second sentence saying "I have a more economic option for you" means I have another option meeting your demand with no extra charges. So it's important to know that we can express things with creating different feelings and additional information. I have to go to work and I get to go to work are not same at all. I need to get better at doing this or I can never do this. And many other examples for encouraging or destructive inner voice. Every time you are speaking to yourself, ask yourself that if you would use the same sentence to someone who you care or you love. Then ask yourself why you would not say it them but you say it to yourself? Are you less valuable person or you care less about yourself? There may be other reasons for that. You have to find it in order to be able to fix it. After finding the reason, keep questioning until getting to the main root or the reason. You will find there is no basis for this conversation, it's just disembarking negative mood, anger or it's the way you use to talk and it's a habit now.

What is your most used vocabulary in your self-talk? What kind of conversation you have with yourself. If you never noticed up to now, from now on you need to pay attention and catch your red hand when you blame yourself during the day. Do you say the same sentence to someone else or do let someone else to tell you that? At the end of the day evaluate how many times you disrespected yourself or blamed yours. Make list of negative words and sentences you use and find a positive one for replacing them. One more thing about self-talk is that some people pretend to have a positive self-talk. It means they start day by saying some artificial sentences and when they are emotionally under pressure, they start bombarding themselves with negative words. Real time conversation is needed not dialogues with no feelings.

Be the best friend of yourself. In words and images provide yourself with bests. There is a trap for us which is comparing ourselves with others. We are watching ourselves all the times even in backstage, but we only see others in their show time. Then we compare our backstage with their show time. People are so good with high personality, character and we are a weirdo. Believe me they are too, you haven't just seen. Generally you shouldn't compare yourself with anyone. Comparing others show time with your backstage is another level of emotional self-sabotage.

There are many positive things about you that you don't feel need to talk about them with yourself. But in fact, you are the most important person who needs to hear about them.

Make a list of things you like about being you, things you did in past and you are proud of them. The things that you are talented about, things that you are blessed with, things that you are thankful for, anything about you and your life that gives you a positive vibe.

Table 3

1. ....
2. ....
3. ....
4. ....
5. ....
6. ....
7. ....
8. ....
9. ....
10. ....
11. ....
12. ....
13. ....
14. ....
15. ....
16. ....
17. ....
18. ....
19. ....
20. ....

Power of repetition and self-talk effect on subconscious.

There are two types of people around you effecting your inner voice. Type one who talk with you in an inspiring way mentioning your positive aspects and reminding you about the things you handled well. Respecting you and making you feel that you are important. And the other type who always keep telling you about your failures and why you cannot do this, you cannot do that. Sometimes they even invent their own creative way to make you feel pity about yourself. Because of long term relationship and power of repetition, both group conversations and behaviors will affect your inner voice. So get rid of the second type as soon as possible. You don't need such a toxic relationship.

Furthermore, positive self-talk and a more optimistic outlook can have other health benefits, including:

Increase vitality

Greater life satisfaction

Improved immune function

Reduced pain

Better cardiovascular health

Better physical well-being

Reduced risk for death

Less stress and distress

Optimists and individuals with more positive self-talk experience these benefits. However, research suggests people with positive self-talk may have mental skills that allow them to solve problems, think differently, and be more efficient at coping with hardships or challenges. This can reduce the harmful effects of stress and anxiety.

External voice

You remember we talked about how our emotions effect our physic and vice versa. Our physics effects our emotions and feelings. There is same situation for voice. Your feelings affect your voice but also your voice can affect your feelings. When you are not confident and have low self-esteem, you slouch and roll your shoulders inward. Your mind and mood controls your muscles and final form of your body. Same is true for muscles controlling form of your voice. If you consciously tune your voice to a confidence voice, with chest voice and not head voice, it will increase your confidence. The same way your confidence increases when you hold your shoulders back and head up. So we will check some techniques to speak with deeper and more confident voice to support our inner voice.

Diaphragm practice

Diaphragm is a muscle under lungs that is involved with breathing and speaking. Diaphragm exercises, not only will help you with better voice but also will help you with breathing practice. To perform this exercise you need to sit on a chair. Sit comfortably, with your knees bent and your shoulders, head and neck relaxed. Place one hand on your upper chest and the other just below your rib cage. This will allow you to feel your diaphragm move as you breathe. Breathe-in slowly through your nose so that your stomach moves out against your hand. The hand on your chest should remain as still as possible. Tighten your stomach muscles, so that your stomach moves back in, as you exhale through pursed lips. Imagine you are blowing a candle off. Later on you will be able to do it without hand and still be aware where your lungs implies the pressure. Then you can try different positions. You can do it laying down and standing as well.

Move your tongue around

With your mouth slightly open, move your tongue around, back and forth. Repeat this exercise for few times. This exercise will help to loosen and relax the muscles at the back of your tongue. Bring your tongue back as much as possible in way that you see your Adams apple going down.

Roll your shoulders and neck

Keeping your shoulders still, slowly rotate your head counterclockwise then clockwise. Do this ten times. Keeping your neck still, rotate your shoulders backward ten times and forward ten times. Coupled together, these exercises will help loosen the muscles around your throat and neck.

Humming

Humming Exercises Stretch Your Vocal Cords. Relax your facial muscles and body. Place the tip of your tongue behind your bottom front teeth. Make "hmmm" sound with your jaw open and your lips closed. Hum notes up and down your range while keeping your mouth closed. Stronger muscles in mouth, throat and diaphragm will help you to have a better voice. Consciously making some changes on muscles involve, will cause to have better voice that will be encouraging and benefiting you mentally.

Visual

Vibration

Introduction

Mental visual activity is something that we do all the times. Actually we don't have a day not doing it. It is one of the steps of creating anything. It's like a lab, we try things there first and we see how does it looks and then we try it out. This process is not for free. You have certain amount of energy for everything. That's why most well-known entrepreneurs have few sets of one certain clothes in one color that they keep putting on every day. Because they don't want to spend any decision on clothes. They have more important decisions to make. They keep their mind busy with less decisions to get better results on their few important decisions. In other words, they simplify their daily chores to put all their mental potentials on their goals and plans. You have certain amount of energy, drive and appetite for visualization. İf you spend your visualization on creating negative things or spend replaying negative memory, then you have no energy left for positive creation neither you have derive for it.

Mental self-image

When you think about anyone, you start picturing them or hearing them mentally. That's how your brain save and recall character and people you know. You remember people by how they look and how they sound. And you do it to yourself as well. You have a picture and voice overall record of yourself which is called self-image. As everything you create in mind and then try it out, also you create yourself first in your mind. If you make realistic changes in your mental image and keep repeating, it will change your believe about yourself and finally you will be it. It can be positive either it can be negative. It's something that many athletes, artists and etc, already are using it. They picture themselves in the shape that they want to be and finally they turn into it. But some people use it to destroy themselves by picture themselves miserable in dramas and finally they get depressed and sick. If it's effecting you this much, why shouldn't you have plan for using it in your favor. Internally and externally can make changes on self-image. Every time you imagine yourself, be sure you see yourself in a healthy and good way. Imagine yourself as a confident character, it will increase your confidence in your real life. In order to improve mental self-image externally, pay attention how you hold your shoulders when you walk or sit. Get use to holding your shoulders back until it gets to be your default mood and everyday walking and sitting is confidence and self-esteem practice for you. In any position you are, pay attention to your body posture and never indulge yourself to slouch or bend. Do adjustments needed for your computer screen, your chair in the office, sit of your car, and other things effecting your posture. Daily exercise is hobby for most of extraordinary people and it helps them in many ways. Besides improving your body, getting healthier, better food digestion, better sleep, good mood and stress release and.... Also it's one important action to take in order to improve self-image. Remember we talked about brain chemicals and happy hormones, exercise is the best for mental health and it will increase your self-image by chemicals released in your brain and also with the changes it will cause in your posture.

Why do we need to visualize

Human being's subconscious works in a very mysterious way and only when we do understand how does it function, then we can overcome it's obstacles consciously, otherwise we have to wait maybe life circumstances put us in a situation that it is not optional anymore to change or not, in order to survival our paradigms should be shifted. Long story short, main reason for not achieving goals and things we wanted, is our own brain not situation or any other thing. It may sound funny or you may ask what is wrong with our brain or if our brain has problem with us? But there is many psychological reasons and explanation for it. One of the main duties of our brain is to protect us consciously and subconsciously. One of the situations that our brain protects us from, is unknown situation. The state that our brain has no information, no previous experience, no connection and no control. You want to change your life and things for you so it will be totally different and new (unknown for subconscious) but your brain protection protocol does not agree with it and says it's not safe to do so. Visualization is the art of familiarizing your subconscious mind with new state that you are about to inter so your subconscious brings down the protection barriers and lets you move forward.

"Imagination is more important than knowledge."

Albert Einstein

Visualizing basics

Present tense

As well talked about it earlier, the main goal of mental image is to make connection with that situation or state. So to make that connection you need to feel it and experience it. Your brain can be tricked and assume the imaginary experience as a real experience if it is visualized in present tense. For brain imaginary past is memory, imaginary future is dream and present in any form is present experience, it can be imaginary or real. From present tense you can create an experience in future and also you can create an experience and replace it with past memory. In clinical psychology there is technique that replaces bad real experience in the past with an imaginary experience to help patient to get over with the bad feeling of that memory. Simply by creating a mental image that Denise the reality or sensibility of that memory. İf you see someone dying in front of your eyes, probably you will not be ok for days or even weeks but you have no idea how many times you have seen people dying in movies or real tragedies in news. They don't create the same feelings and it's possible to exchange or overwrite them. Same manipulation can be implemented to our future vision to get our future out of random circumstances. From the present time you have access to past and future in mind and on the other hand, whatever you keep in mind from the past and whatever you created in mind for the future will effect whatever you do in the present time. So it is important to remember that there is difference between daydreaming and visualization

All senses involved

One factor to make an image sensible and real is to do it in present time but that's not all. İn experience there are other senses involved as same as vision. Hearing, smelling tasting and touching should be involved in this visualization. It should be vivid and clear. But if at first you couldn't make it, you can divide it into few steps. First create the visual part and see it to end then second time visualize it with voices added, and other senses step by step until it has almost all factors of real experience. Repeat it as much as you can, let your subconscious get use to it and start working on it even when you are sleeping. Last thing that we are thinking about it before sleeping is the most probably the thing we will subconsciously be busy with it while sleeping, even in some cases in some forms it will appear in our night dream. So what a great time to think about something positive, and give our mind a productive task for the night to sleep on it.

Realistic vision

There is a very important point to have your visions real which is visualizing through your body. What I'm trying to say is that you never see your face in reality unless you are in front of mirror or something that you can see reflection of your face. In a vivid vision you see things through your eyes not seeing yourself full body from outside. Voices better to sound real as well, like having background voice, city ham or anything making it realistic depending on what is and where is the image. For example if you imagine yourself wining Oscar, add the voice of people clapping and etc. Touch the reward in your imagination, notice the smoothness and temperature of it. Kiss it and imagine the smell of metal. If it helps, before starting visualization have similar materials and do the touching and smelling to help you imagine it more clearly.

Visualizing and manifestation techniques

-369: If you believe in numerology, there is technique called 369. It's easy, write down whatever you want to manifest and do visualizing it: 3 times in the morning, 6 times during the day and 9 times in the evening. Nicola Tesla is the inventor of this technique. Even you don't believe in numerology this technique is going to be helpful for you because of number of times you repeat your goals. Every day for 18 times and it will accelerate settling your goals in your subconscious mind.

-Journaling is another useful technique. You can have notebook with yourself or a digital notebook on your phone but paper and pen is more recommended. Write down your thoughts, dreams, goals and anything coming to you and you want them.

-Gratitude journal: one of great manifesting tools is gratification. Keeping a gratitude journal will boost your present feelings and your mindset for better. Write down everything that you are grateful for in life. Every day at night add any good things that happened to you during the day. Once in a while review this journal and remind yourself that how blessed you are and still there is a lot yet to come. You will add them to your journal when the time comes for it.

-Listing: You can make list of your goals on piece of paper and read it every morning before starting the day and every night before going to bed. It can be everything you want no matter how small or how big. It can be learning how to drive car up to traveling to moon in next centuries.

-There is a method called "pillow method". In this method you write down your dreams before going to sleep and put them under your pillow. Of course you can put it anywhere else, the point of this method is to write your dream before sleeping so you can go to bed with clear mind and leave your brain with that positive idea to the sleeping time. You will have more positive bed time and subsequently a better morning afterwards.

-Creating a vision board. It's one of the easiest manifestation techniques to practice. Clarify your goals and vision, gather materials, find images and objects that represent your vision, arrange your materials on board and then place your board where you will see it often.

-The two cup method: If you'd like to try the two cup method though, simply get out two cups. Fill one cup, and label it with your current situation (i.e. single, lonely, or however you're feeling right now). Label the empty cup with the situation you hope to manifest (i.e. loving relationship). Once you have the cups labeled, reflect for a moment on your current situation and how you will feel once you reach your desired outcome. Holding onto that positive feeling, pour the water from the current situation cup to the desired situation cup. Drink all the water in this desired situation cup, and rip up the label from the current situation cup. Hold onto the label from the desired situation cup, and know that you're now attracting the situations that leads you to whatever your desired outcome is.

-Visualization before falling sleep. When you go to bed, start doing self-hypnosis (muscle by muscle from head to toe, feel and release from tension. Make sure all your muscles in body are loosen and relaxed) then visualize achieving your goals until you fall asleep.

-55 x 5 Method. The 55 x 5 method is a manifestation method to practice positive affirmations. All you need to do to practice the 55 x 5 method is think of the thing you want to manifest, and turn it into an affirmation. Then, write down this affirmation 55 times every day for five days in a row. For manifestation techniques to really work, remember to stay present and keep your head focused on your desired outcome.

-Worry Box: Sometimes we first need to clear our mind from negative though before visualization.

Write down your fears and anxieties on a little pieces of paper, and keep them in a sealed box or container. When you're able to, discard all of those fears and anxieties by either shredding them or burning them in the fireplace.

-Congratulations technique: mentally experiencing the moment of achieving a certain goal tricks your mind to believe that the goal is bound to happen and it's possible.

-Letter from future self: the letter from Future Self Manifestation Strategy consists of writing a letter from your future self to your present self. In this letter, you will discuss the goals you have accomplished in great detail and how rich your life has become.

-Fake it until you make it: this is one of the most known techniques for tricking your mind about who you are and how do you feel about yourself and everything else. You will play role of your desired character until gradually you will become that character.

-Mirror method: the mirror method is a manifestation technique that involves looking into a mirror and repeating affirmations to yourself. This is one of the more popular manifestation methods that helps to program your subconscious mind with positive beliefs about yourself and your ability to achieve your goals. You look into the mirror and say, "I am _" (fill in the blank with your goal or desire).

-Manifestation box: it is a special box that you fill with items that represent your goals and desires. This helps to focus your energy on what you want and makes it more likely to come into your life. Just make sure to choose items that really resonate with you and what you want to achieve. Your future self will thank you!

-Feng-Shui: Feng-Shui is the ancient Chinese art of placement. It's based on the belief that our environment affects our energy, and so by arranging our surroundings in certain ways, we can attract different things into our lives. For a successful manifestation, it's important to create a space that is clean, clutter-free, and peaceful. This will allow you to focus your energy on what you want to achieve and make it more likely to happen.

-Nothing to lose mindset: this is one thing that always keeps you away from fear of loss. For example if you have stress about your career, while you are still working in a company find another position in other organizations that you can fit and even once in a while apply for some positions which you don't have intention to go. Now you have different opportunities that you can take if you lose your current job. this will take away your fear of losing your job. When you don't resonate stress and fear, universe works for you and fix your current situation. Fearlessness is key factor to attract positive things.

-3 scene technique: before going to sleep, do self-hypnosis and then start visualization in there steps.

1. Visualize the problem and watch in your mind for 2 minutes with every details.

2. Visualize taking action to solve the problem for 2 minutes.

3. Visualize the moment that the problem is solved and experience happiness and feeling after the problem is solved. It also will be two minutes.

It will make a track to follow for your subconscious mind.

-Law of attraction: our brain categories things into pleasure and pain. Every possibility you consider for future can be pleasurable or painful. You can be fulfilled by fear or joy. If most of times, you are thinking about how good it will feel when a certain thing is archived, then your main resonation to universe is positive and universe will reflect it back to you. If you are focused on awful feeling of losing of things, then universe will help you to experience it. So try to think about positive possibility and visualize positive things to attract them. You are the one who orders, your subconscious and universe follow what you have ordered and help you to achieve it.

-Examine Your Why: it's an important manifestation technique is to examine your why. This is an important step in how to define your intentions for manifestation, and it ensures that you are manifesting the right things, for the right reasons. If you're not manifesting for the right reasons, the above manifestation strategies simply won't work!

In some of these techniques you read, there were objects mentioned like pillow, cup and other objects. It may sound crazy but let me briefly explain it. When you have something in mind that is considered as worry or whatever and you imagine it by using and object, your brain considers that object as that thought or part of it. Whatever you do with that object, it will effect that thought as well. If it helps, imagine you make physical copy of mental thing. It's a worry called X. You have one X in mind and one X you have in your hand. You have same feelings and emotions for both of them. There is two objects (one mental and physical) with one feeling Link. Now two objects status can make changes on feelings about X. When you get rid of physical X and feel relief, you feel relief about X or less worried despite remembering there is a X in mind.

We have gone through all these techniques to get some materials for starting our project. Get back to methods and read them again if you need and choose few of them to put in use in the project. You don't have to use all of them and actually you shouldn't use too many techniques at the same time. We will have visualization for sure and you can add ones you more believe it. Whichever you think it will work for you or you feel more comfortable with, would be a good option for you.

Visual Life
Project

This project would be the biggest and final home-work in this book. You will create everything around you and yourself as well. Before rushing to project, let's take our times and understand why we want to do this, what is the point. Also it would be good to have a review on principles and techniques that we learnt. We are going to implant an idea of the life you want to live into deeper levels of your mind. We want implant it so deep that doubts of its possibility fades away from your subconscious and then you start resonate with abundance frequency and start enlarging your mental capacities for wealth. As you continue repeating this practice, characteristics of imaginary you will effect characteristics of you until they match. How good you practice will says how far you can go. Your life standards will start to change. Your mindset will start to shift and gradually your life will move toward the life you have created in your mind.

Imagine you are living in a dream land and there is no limit for anything. Where you can have every real thing you want. You have no money issue. Nobody can reject you, you get everything you choose. What would your life look like? Every day you will spend few minutes of your day in the life you are creating in this project.

This mental design should be bought by your mind so avoid too much exaggeration and things not possible based on this world and physic rules. Think big but not in way that your brain doubts that's possibility. For example imagine yourself having your favorite car but it's not acceptable to imagine having spaceship. The day you really owned every luxury and expensive car you wanted, then it would be acceptable to visualize private jet and after that you can visualize spaceship, but for now the dream of a nice car is good. To make as much as vivid, we need to cover some topics as follow

Your belongings

During this visualization you will need few background views and places for your scenes which will stand for your financial situation. You will need to have a design for living place, neighborhood, office, car, and etc. Make it in such way that you will be able to remember the same scenes every-time. You won't change your home or car during the practices. You will use same images for a while until it gets bolder and bolder in your mind. You can use views that you are familiar with and also it inspires you. It worth reminding again that you will involve all your senses. When you get in to your car hear the voice of closing the door, imagine the touching steering wheel and all other things. Smell of fabric or perfume on you. Put-in use some creativity. Maybe you put on a music or you turn on the radio. Do whatever it takes to make it as vivid as possible. You have to be really good at creating these things because your brain will not accept it otherwise.

Your health and self-image

You will be the main role in this manifestation so you need to use a mental image of yourself. The question is that how would you be in that future time. Shape of body and health condition. Sometimes regarding internal addiction or negative mood, we visualize ourselves in deathbed or funeral. It also caused because of not receiving expected attention in real life so we do it in imagination by seeing ourselves dead or sick and people are regretting not taking us serious. It's dumb as hell, and it really gives distractive message to your body. See yourself in your healthy and fit mood and keep your self-image as positive as possible. Spend some time on designing your physic and body form. Regarding self-visualization principles we talked about before, you will see through your eyes in all time. You can go in front of mirror in your vision but besides that no self-image from outside.

Your relationships

Create characters that you want spending time with. Even name them, so every time you will see yourself with that person on that scenes you already created. You will make a memory with imaginary you and other characters in imaginary scene. Every day we may interacting with many people and we have met thousands of them. Some of them were already chosen like family members but the others are chosen by us. We accepted them between thousands of people we have met. We let some of them go and we keep some of them for long. How do we decide and choose? What if we have habit of staying in comfort zone in relationships? We have filling of not being Worthy for relationship with some kind of people. We may have fear of rejection. What if we have gotten used to specific type of people which is toxic for us? And the final question, what if we can manipulate all these patterns by imagination? We can create positive characters and spend time with them and finally it will affect our relationships in real life. It will change our standards in relationships. This is the part you will use inner voice the most. During the visualizing interacting with imaginary characters there will be positive, productive, respectful conversations and expressions.

Your hobbies

In real time life, you are not just working, studying or with family. You have some inspiring activities which will be the spice of this project. If you have never afford to do skydiving and you really wanted to do it, then it's time to do. Having motivation and drive to get going on life would be really helpful. Regardless of financial limits chose whatever you enjoy doing in your free time and repeat doing it with self-image you have created.

Your occupation

This part will be completed after reading final chapter. You will apply the principles used in previous subjects. There is no limitation like financial, geographic location, and educational. Every business is possible but it should be the one you meant to do, you love to do and you are borne to do. That's why we need to finish this part after final chapter but for previous subjects you can start designing scenes, characters, belongings, and hobbies.

Best time to practice regarding the frequency and brain waves, is immediately after waking up in the morning and before sleeping at night. This practice should be performed with details in joyful and exciting way so it should end up with emotional reaction of brain during the Visualization, otherwise it doesn't sound that much real and distinguishable experience for your mind. Another thing that can be helpful is to get some materials that you use in the visualization. Nothing expensive or fancy. Just try to have some objects in both lives. For example if in your life project your hobby is playing golf, buy a golf ball.

Taking

Action

What is my way?

After mastering creation of positive visions and voices you still need one more thing which is action. Your mental positive creation should get a physical form as well and that cannot be done without action. There are wide ranges of things to do. You can start doing anything, but you didn't come this far to do something ordinary and fit in mediocracy. Doing things that you don't meant to do. Doing things you are not interested, you suffer doing it for promising pleasure at the end. Trading your time and energy for only living. Simply being alive, to enjoy the food you need to get hungry, to enjoy the rest you should get tired, everything pleasurable thing in this life has to be paid by pain. One unit pleasure costs at least one unit pain. There is only one thing that changes this deal for good and that's love. Love blinds you for pain and process difficulties and lets you see pleasure from starting to the end. Human being can love many things, another human being and so on. Being in love is good but being in love with what you create, is another level. This is what makes human being different than every existing thing in this universe. We are not just a creature or transformer. We are creators and if we fall in love with creating something, we will reborn to live our second lives. Not just a creature but also a creator. Ok enough big words and let's get to work. In order to do that, first you need to know who you are? What do you want to get? Who do you want to be? What is your pass? And…..

So first you need to know who you are. Who you are doesn't mean what is your favorite color or favorite dish. What you are good at doing? What you are not good at doing? How do you response to different circumstances emotionally. How are you in relationship with others? What excites you? What makes you sad? What are your fears in life? And so on.

In modern day world is a little bit difficult to find the answer of this question because of educational system we have all gone through, but it is not impossible. We have to differentiate who we are, who we are programed to be and who we are pretending to be. It sounds a little bit confusing but let me explain in my way. If we assume from tomorrow on, no one will be permitted and able to know other people's job and no one will has right to inform anyone about his job, how many people will keep doing what they were doing? In most part of the world there are certain jobs that if you do not manage to get that career, you are not accepted as a successful person in that society. So we can say most of us are living the life that does not belong to us. We have to find out, but how?

There are many psychology tests to help which you can find over the internet but there is a better way for that which will help us to find our talents and passion.

Talents

Have you ever seen a two years old kid paying with toys and worrying if people seeing him would like the way he or she pays or not? What he or she is doing with toys is important or the brand of the toy? Dose that kid lose confidence because of brand of his diaper? Does he or she choose the toy according to the other people's opinion? It is still not manipulated and pure, minding his own business. Still not bombarded with "you can't, you shouldn't, that's bad, that's wrong, that's not for you". To know ourselves better, we need to remember who we really were before growing up. When we were not educated, when were not normalized yet, when we used to do things that we wanted to do no matter what, when we were who we were. We need to travel to our childhood. Make your childhood character study case and start gathering information about it. Which games you used to play more? Which cartoons were your favorites? Cartoon about football or cars? What was the school subjects you used to get best results with minimum effort? Which subjects were your nightmares? Find your school reports and read them. For me, those were the most terrifying peace of papers at the time but now I can use them to understand myself better. For example my school report cards say "don't get involved in things demanding too much mathematic skills". There are many kinds of intelligence. Some people are very good with numbers and calculation, some others are good with visuals and drawings. Some people can distinguish voices apart from each other regarding that they had no training for it. Some people are born as an athlete. Finally all these smart kids has been convinced by family and society that if they want to be successful, they need to be doctor, lawyer or at least engineer. Only god knows how many Beethovens are teaching math in school instead of dealing with music, how many Picassos are in hospital instead of drawing, how many Marlon Brandons are in engineering jobs. Your childhood information will help you to know yourself before normalization process.

Make a list of things that you think you are talented in. it can be anything that You can perform well. For example, cooking, driving, drawing …

Table 4

1..

2..

3..

4..

5..

6..

7..

8..

9..

10..

11..

12..

13..

14..

15..

16..

17..

18..

19..

20..

Passion

Whenever tip of your nose is scratching, you scratch whole your body except tip of your nose, you won't feel relieved. You have to scratch the right location. This is same for passion you can try hard and suffer doing many things and even you can be good at doing some of them as well but if you want to get devoted, get lost in the moments, feeling of cannot wait for sun to rise to start a day, to feel as same as 3 years old kid waking up in joy and running to play with his toys first thing in the morning, you have to find your scratching field. It doesn't happen for everyone majority of people keep doing things that they have been told to do. If you want to live full life and not just simply be alive, then you have to find what you want. Also your passion can be tracked from your childhood up to your present. There are some memories from your childhood which are bolder that the others. I don't mean like birthday memories. Memories involve certain types of activity. Your most excited moments doing something. It can be a journey to museum or zoo. It can be building something or fixing part of building with your father. It can be the day you burned your first cooking meal. Also there is a documented thing saying a lot about your childhood thought and interests which is your drawing papers. If you find them you can see what you were drawing the most. Get your clues from your childhood and get back to the present. There are things that can be found in your childhood and there are things that you have discovered after growing up. So taking look at our present time also is needed. Especially our free time activities. The things we do only because we enjoy doing it. Type of books we read. Movies that we watch. Google or Instagram knows you better than you probably but they won't give your information to you. See which pages you follow the most. Take a pen (not pensil) write down twenty things you want to do in life. Before writing the item consider this. Money is not an issue, you are financially independent. You have everything you need and you want. You will do it only because you enjoy doing and you want it to be done. What would be those things?

Table 5

1. ....

2. ....

3. ....

4. ....

5. ....

6. ....

7. ....

8. ....

9. ....

10. ....

11. ....

12. ....

13. ....

14. ....

15. ....

16. ....

17. ....

18. ....

19. ....

20. ....

Give your talent a chance to accompany your passion

Put both tables besides each other and see if you can find any resemblance between them. Any item in talent somehow related to an item in the passion table. Your talents are your resources, if there is anything that for doing it you can use your talents, it will compound your progress and in a very short time you will get things done. Imagine your talent as one hand and passion as another one. With both hands cooperating together, you can accomplish a lot. Your mind is holding your talents and your heart is holding your passion. If you put both your mind and heart on doing anything, it would be an extraordinary work. Money also will come after you because you are doing something extraordinary but you cannot do something extraordinary for money. It means if you forget about money at first and start doing what excites you and you are good at doing it, rapidly you will grow and you will be a master of what you are doing, so you will be receiving equal as you provide, as much as value you add. But if your first priority is money, then you will look for a place that they pay more for your time in a 9-5 job. Then you will enter into a rat race which will leave you with almost nothing at your 60s or 70s. You have nothing at destination and you couldn't enjoy the ride. This is how the work life is, go after your dreams and enjoy every day taking step toward it while financially growing as well or go after money at first. Start doing something you don't like which will not help you to do anything outstanding and finally fail to get financially free.

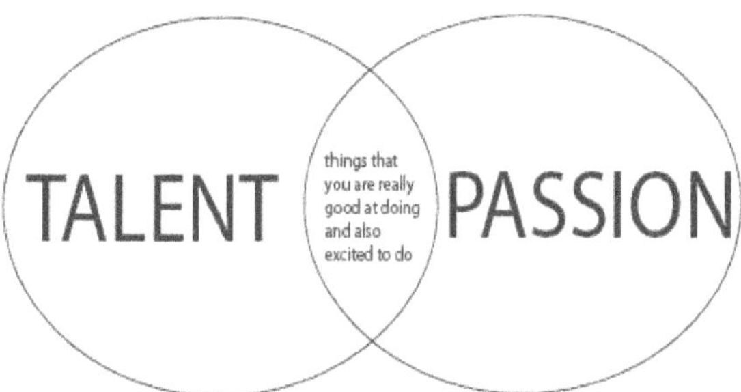

Supply and demand

Find what your talent and passion can change for others. One thing that you should visualize in your life project about your career, is that you should see other people benefiting whatever you are doing. Jose Silva creator of 3 scene technique, has divided the practice this way. See the problem in your mind with details, see yourself taking action to solve it and in the last scene watching problem solved also see how other people benefits from your solution. Anything you can do and you want to which also can optimize things for better results. What is that needed to be changed in it to provide a better result for other people?

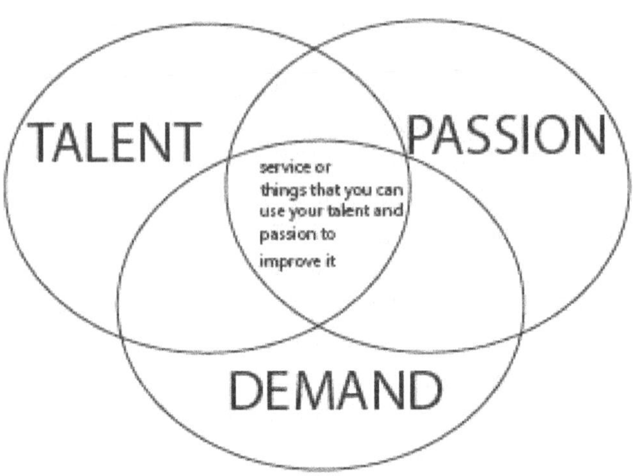

Plan

Have a clear vision of your goal

One of the great quotes that I have read in my life is "everything has been created twice, once in imagination of man-kind then in physical form". When you are learning a new language in order to be able to pronounce a word fluently you need to have a clear vocal imagination of that word in your mind. If in the middle of pronouncing you stop to think of next part of the word, then you failed to pronounce it. If you are drawing something, you need to have a visual imagination of final result, divide it to smaller objects and then connect them to each other. Same is true for your life. You should clarify what you want, which direction you want to go and what things you need to pick up on your way. Your goal may change on your way or it will get shifted for a better one but you cannot start with no goal in mind. Your goal should be detailed otherwise your mind will throw it away. It is not real and understandable. That's why in life-project we will try to cover different aspects of your life with details. Write down your net income, your position, and everything you want.

Set realistic milestones

Every goal is achievable if you can manage to divide it to achievable steps toward that goal. When you go to climb a mountain, you don't just head toward the summit. If you do, you will get lost, you will get disappointed and stuck somewhere. You have to distinguish stations that you have on the way and how to go to each station or hill until all these stations end in the pick.

This is also correct for life plan. First you define the main goal, then you divide it to milestones and then you start to move on the track. Time and distance of each stations are important. This is where planning skills will be revealed. Milestone can be as easy as not creating any motivation to achieve or as difficult as discouraging to follow toward. If you fail to set a right milestone, you will fail to achieve your goal. So you need to be accurate about time and distance of each milestone. One day you will find out that final goal itself, was a milestone for a bigger goal.

Design a system

Now we have clarified what we have (talent and passion) and what we want (goal and milestones). We need a system between our input and output. We have to set routines and create habits by the time. Which actions will lead you toward that milestones? Details of process, repetition, and daily plan for it. Write down the actions you need to take in order to get each milestone. For example if you are learning a new language and you have written how many words each month you will learn, how many new sentence structure you will master, then you have clarify which method and materials you will use to get it done. Write process with details and stick to it until getting it done and don't forget to celebrate every big and small achievements.

Get rid of your mental obstacles

Debug your wrong believes and thoughts about growing. You should have understood by now that you cannot have intention to grow and not to grow at the same time. Find out what are the reasons that your subconscious mind is having to stop you from success. Don't insist on doing hard work on somethings without convincing your subconscious mind to accompany you. The life project you have, will help you to make connection between your dream life and your subconscious, but there are some wrong beliefs rooted in your past that needs to be found and healed.

Unworthiness and shyness

Feeling unworthy is one of the most important reasons for not growing and improving. Main reason for feeling unworthiness comes from depression. This is not gonna leave you free until you solve this problem. You may never notice when it happened. Most of us are dealing with depression, anxiety or stress in some level which effects all areas of our lives, personal growth included. It may be caused by a boring daily routine, trauma, abuse, neglect or any other difficult situation in the past. Does it need to change life style? Does it need to try new things? Does it need help and medication? Do whatever it takes to get rid of it. Hiding is not a solution and never was and nobody is gonna solve it for you without you asking for it. You will do it yourself, if you need expert to help, ask for it and do it now. You need the feeling of worthiness to be able to receive good life. Also being shy and fear of standing out will be a great obstacle on the way. You may had bad memories, being humiliated in the past and etc. which makes you feel safe when you hide behind and no one see you. Face them today and let them go.

Fear and guilt

Another wrong believe that we have about abundance is that wealthy people have too much problem in life. This crime towards us happened by watching too much crap movies, get another peoples wrong mindset, childhood wrong evaluations, not having close connection with someone wealthy and really understanding it. For sure you have seen movies in which there is poor, good, happy and lovely character or characters which you make emotional bound with them and on the other side there is a rich savage character with too many problems which you hate. Your emotional bounds and hatred in that movie will be linked to other poor and rich guys in real life. These movies will finally change your definition about wealthy and poor. As where as you don't want to be savage and stuck with problems, you will prevent yourself from getting wealthy. Many other things around you will affect your believe about wealth. You may also can be taught that people who are wealthy for sure have done something wrong or illegal. Someone should lose something in life so you can win it, is another wrong concept about wealth. Everyone has a mental wealth capacity and they will only have wealth in real life as much as their mental wealth capacity. It is not your fault if they didn't get as much as you got. You better always help but never feel responsible for anyone's poverty.

You can carry some wrong believe from childhood without knowing. Let me set an imaginary example. You are a kid sent to school every morning by taxi or private driver while watching other kids getting into school bus, laughing, having good time together. You feel lonely on the way thinking what are they doing, by passage of time you will link your life standards with loneliness and you may keep it for Long time. You are always trying to be ordinary person preferring bus to private service because it feels happier.

Religious beliefs

Some beliefs or superstitious thought saying that living very poor life is gonna be spiritual and you will end up in heaven. You may not agree with it right now and say it is nonsense but somewhere deep down it may still effects your thoughts. You may never thought about it but it doesn't mean you don't believe in it. You can have totally different conscious beliefs and subconscious beliefs. I have experienced it many times, and there is a one memory that I never forget. I'm in my early 20s, having a little arrogance like most people at that age and deeply into philosophy. Only period of my life that I claimed being atheist. I'm not talking about religions being right or wrong, I'm talking about two different religions beliefs in one person at the same time. One weekend like most of the others, we hit the road to climb a mountain in a cold winter day. Everywhere covered under the snow. We start climbing to top and climbed most of it. Everything was like a normal hiking day until we get to the point that snow is up to belly, difficult to go forward and more difficult to go back. We decided to pass that cap of snow anyway but when we were in the middle of that shallow zone, we heard the cracking voice of ice in lower layers. If it breaks, we will all go down with avalanche. I looked down to valley and noticed nothing survives that, then as an atheist I looked to sky and sincerely asked God to take me out of this alive. Why God came first thing in to my mind was because I was still believing in god no matter what I was claiming or how many logical reasons I had for evolution. I was still a believer. Now you may claim you don't have poor mindset believe but you need to examine yourself in different situations.

Positive beliefs for growing

Finally, you need the mindset that feels good about wealth, believes deeply that money cannot corrupt you, being wealthy is good, you can easily deal with problems, you deserve a fortunate life, you can only help others when you sort out things for yourself first, rich people doesn't go to hell, better to live in abundance rather than normality.

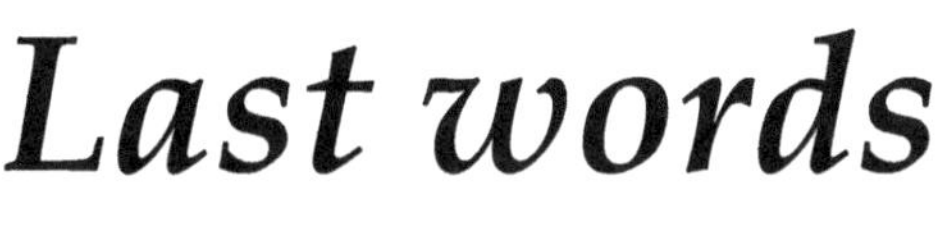

Last words

İf you are reading this part without skipping any pervious part, you have got the overall idea, you have understood what is going on inside your skull when you are thinking, you know thought are not just a thoughts but resonating signals, you have learned the important principles for visualization, you learned techniques how to practice and you already have started additional homework Which will assist your main project. You have made your mind about doing this and that's why you come up to final words. From now on, your main part of journey starts. Up to here, it was all preparation. Temptation and fear will be walking with you in this way. They are only able to do something to you if you let them to do so. Your internal addiction habits, negative thoughts, anger, and other excuses to get a small dose of misery hormones are still around. Destructive habits, fear of change pulling you back to be the way you used to be. İt's not easy to give up daily indulgence or walking away from some relationships, staying out of comfort zone or accepting there are things that you will not experience anymore. İt's not gonna be easy just because you know where to start. But you have everything you need to do this. Everything comes with a price, good days as well. Now it is time to tune your life by tuning your thoughts. It is time to positive creation. Positive visual vibration and positive vocal vibration.

Imagine you are starting a new position in a film industry. In this position you are the writer, designer, actor, director, producer and all other roles needed to prepare the film. You have your normal life and also the role in this film that you will be playing it in your imagination. This film will be written in 40 episodes at first and then can be extended for as long as you want. The rules and principles that we studied about visualization in previous chapters, will be followed. The main role of the film (which is you) regardless of what he or she is doing, is a person surrounded by wealth, health and positive people. The way things happen to you, how others talk with you, and what is your position in that relationships and communities, all should be positive and beneficial. You are never short in money for doing anything. You are in healthy and fit body shape. You don't do anything for money, you already have it but you are in love making change in something specific. See yourself being with character you wish to have and make it clear in scenes how you take care of others and benefit them. Make a list of other positive characteristics and put them in plan.

Write down 40 days routine and stick to it. You can add things later but main activities should be clarified. If you can, write a short scenarios in advance for each day with scenes and characters involved and keep doing it until you can remember all of them clearly like a real life memory. You can also add thing by project progress.

While project is under progress, spread previous tasks through this 40 days and have some actions in real life. Check Table1 and see how many of those five items already is done. If you haven't taken action, you should do it until the end of this 40 days. Set a day and time for them below. Items from Table2 should be done regularly until turning into habit. And Table3 also shouldn't be forgotten until you change your vocabulary toward yourself for a more positive self-talk.

Your visual life project will affect your real life. It depends on how good you perform this project and how much consistency you spend doing it. How good you consider principles, is important. Go back to previous parts and check anything you need to review and then get back.

Day example

Visual Project: I will have a walk with my partner in central park talking about our new investment then I will get on my mustang heading to dinner party with friends.

Present life: I will reserve a table for myself in my favorite restaurant.

Day 1

....

....

....

....

....

....

....

....

Day 2

....

....

....

....

....

....

....

....

Day 3

....
....
....
....
....
....
....
....

Day 4

....
....
....
....
....
....
....
....

Day 5

....
....
....
....
....
....
....
....

Day 6

....

....

....

....

....

....

....

....

Day 7

....

....

....

....

....

....

....

....

Day 8

....

....

....

....

....

....

....

....

Day9

....
....
....
....
....
....
....
....

Day 10

....
....
....
....
....
....
....
....

Day 11

....
....
....
....
....
....
....
.... LAST WORDS

Day 12

....

....

....

....

....

....

....

....

Day 13

....

....

....

....

....

....

....

....

Day 14

....

....

....

....

....

....

....

....

Day 15

....

....

....

....

....

....

....

....

Day 16

....

....

....

....

....

....

....

....

Day 17

....

....

....

....

....

....

.... ■ LAST WORDS......

Day 18

··
··
··
··
··
··
··
····················

Day 19

··
··
··
··
··
··
··
····················

Day 20

··
··
··
··
··
··
··
····················

Day 21

Day 22

Day 23

Day 24

Day 25

Day 26

Day 27

Day 28

Day 29

Day 30

....

....

....

....

....

....

....

....

Day 31

....

....

....

....

....

....

....

....

Day 32

....

....

....

....

....

....

....

....

Day 33

Day 34

Day 35

Day 36

Day 37

Day 38

Day 39

....

....

....

....

....

....

....

....

Day 40

....

....

....

....

....

....

....

....

www.ingramcontent.com/pod-product-compliance
Lightning Source LLC
LaVergne TN
LVHW010539200726
843506LV00013B/2876